Vampire Animals

Written by
Helen Harvey

Ransom

Contents

Vampires

Everybody knows about vampires. You can meet vampires in films or in books.

People say vampires sleep during the day and are awake at night. They have two sharp fangs to suck blood.

Count Dracula is a vampire in a book written by Bram Stoker.

Vampires are not real.

But some animals look or act like vampires.

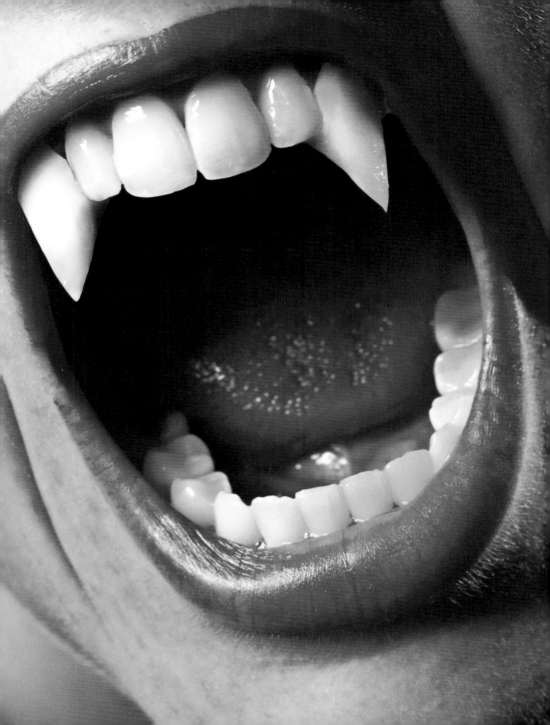

Vampire bats

Vampire bats hunt at night. In the daytime, they sleep in caves.

Vampire bats feed on blood. They don't feed on anything else.

These bats have sharp front teeth. They use these teeth to bite animals such as cows and horses.

The bats then drink their blood.

Some vampire bats will bite and drink the blood of humans.

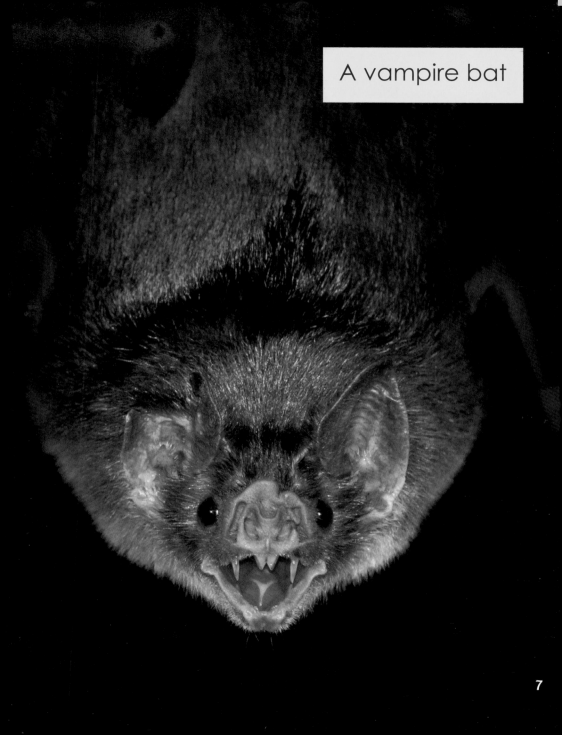

A vampire bat

Vampire squid

The vampire squid is part of the squid family. It looks as if it is wearing a dark red cape.

Vampire squid are not dangerous. They do not eat living things. They feed on dead animals and small matter floating in the ocean.

Vampire squid are not very big. They are only about fifteen centimetres across.

9

A vampire finch

Vampire finches

Vampire finches live in places without much water.

The vampire finches peck the bodies of much bigger birds, called boobies. This makes the boobies' bodies bleed.

Then the vampire finches can drink the boobies' blood.

A booby

Lamprey

This is a lamprey. Some people call it a vampire fish.

It looks like an eel but it is a fish.

The lamprey has a mouth but it has no jaws. It cannot open or close its mouth.

The mouth of the lamprey is like a suction cup. The lamprey has many small teeth in its mouth.

The mouth fixes on to a fish. Then the teeth cut, or rasp, into the skin of fish.

The fish bleeds and the lamprey feeds on the blood.

The mouth of a lamprey

Dracula ants

This is a Dracula ant.

Dracula ants feed on blood.

The ants bite into their own young and drink their blood.

Dracula ants do not kill their babies. So the babies can still grow into adult Dracula ants.

Vampire crabs

This is a vampire crab. Vampire crabs have bright yellow eyes and purple or orange bodies.

They don't suck blood, but eat plants and insects.